AF372184

Hilda the Hen

This book belongs to: _______________

Copyright© 2023. All rights reserved.

No part of this publication may be reproduced, distributed, or transmitted in any form or by any means, including photocopying, recording, or other electronic or mechanical methods, without the prior written permission of the publisher, except in the case of brief quotations embodied in critical reviews and certain other non-commercial uses permitted by copyright law.

First published in 2023 with an exclusive licence from the authors to CHEETAH® Purrrrrrr Publishing, an imprint of CHEETAH® Toys & More, LLC (CHEETAH®).

Contact us: 1-860-781-1276, 1-876-909-6311 (WhatsApp),
info@mycheetahacademy.com; paulettetrowers@yahoo.com

ISBN-13: 979-8-3303-5046-9
ISBN-10: 8-3303-5046-9

Dear CHEETAH® family:

Our little books were specifically created to help our early readers master their decoding skills and build reading fluency. The repetitive use of high-frequency words, word families, decodable words, rhymes, and vivid illustrations facilitates this process. Our stories complement the objectives and content highlighted in the Jamaica Early Childhood Curriculum Guide and the Ministry of Education and the Grade I National Standards Curriculum of the Ministry of Education and Youth.

In journeying through our series, our little ones will develop a deeper awareness of and appreciation for our Jamaican culture. Our books also have universal appeal, as any early reader can identify with the characters, events and subjects in our texts. Readers will get enjoy the stories, build vocabulary, and exercise critical thinking by engaging in the activities at the end of each story.

Additionally, as a precursor to our series, or as a support to it, we have created a decodable 'sentence strip' book for very young readers and those who require more scaffolding.

Happy reading!

CHEETAH®

Chasing and capturing your dreams with you.

C-DER™
CHEETAH Decodable & Early Readers
Each letter is like a piece of a story puzzle. Let's go! Let's place the words together.

My decodable words:

hen, Ken, pen, beg, low,
slow, get, let, wet

Letter sound:

- consonant sounds /h/ and /l/ in the initial, medial and final positions in words

Word families: 'en', 'ow', 'eg', 'et'

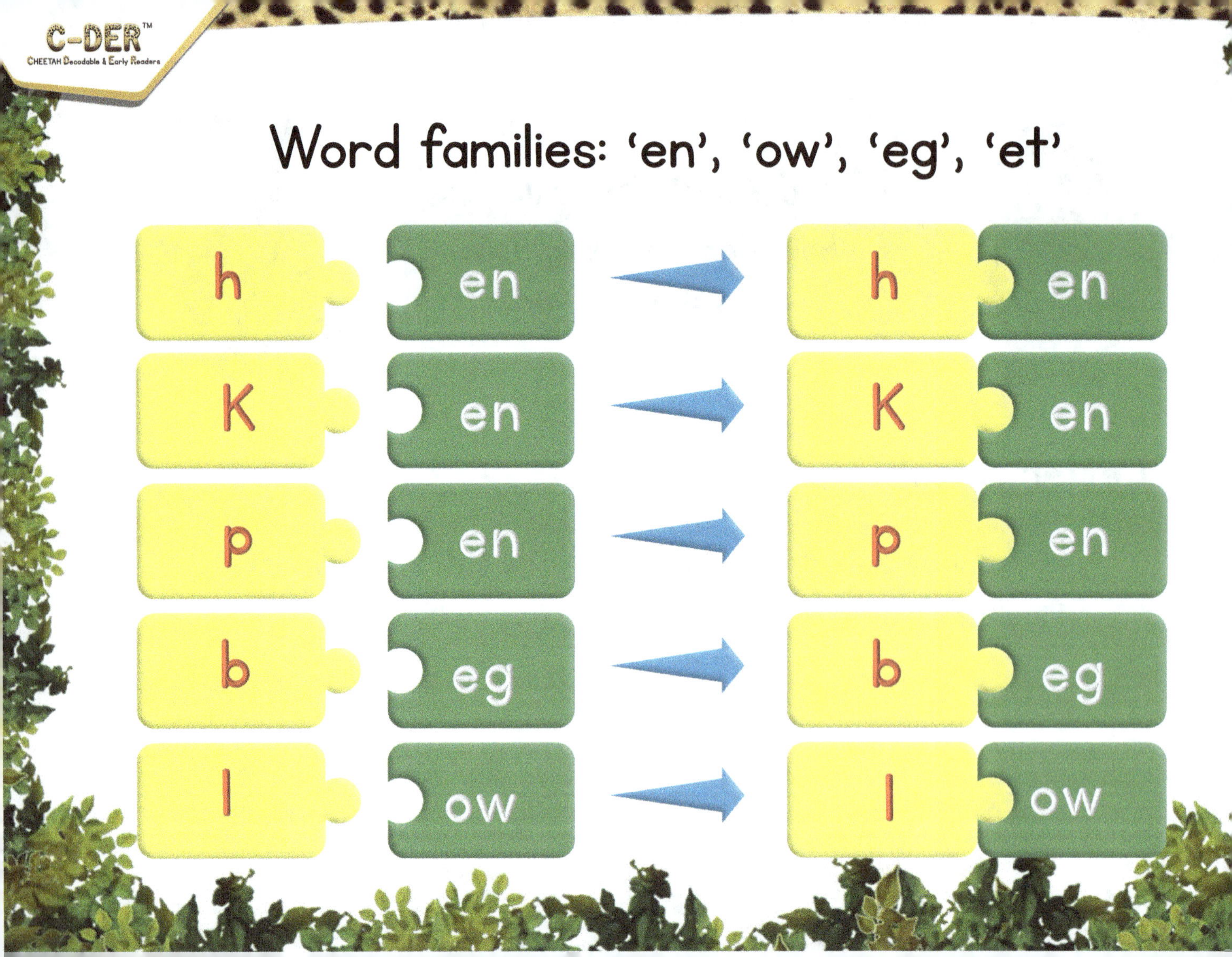

C-DER
CHEETAH Decodable & Early Readers

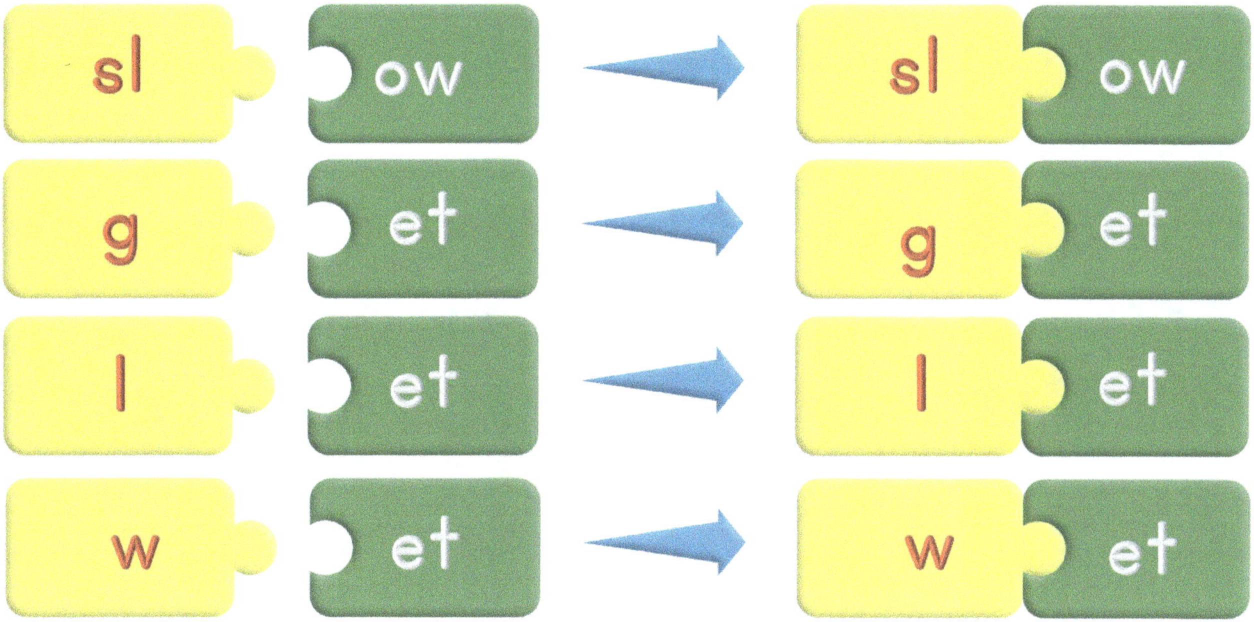

sl
ow
sl ow

g
et
g et

l
et
l et

w
et
w et

C-DER
CHEETAH Decodable & Early Readers
1

Hilda the Hen

I love to visit Hilda the hen.

She sits in the hay in her little pen.

Hilda cannot fly as high as other birds.

I wonder why.

C-DER™
CHEETAH Decodable & Early Readers
3

She does not fly fast. She does not fly slow.

She does not fly far, and she stays very low.

Hilda walks from place to place,

and she does not like to race.

4

C-DER
CHEETAH Decodable & Early Readers
5

Hilda loves to eat white rice.

She seems to think that rice is nice.

Hilda the hen also loves to eat seeds.

She looks for them among the weeds.

C-DER™
CHEETAH Decodable & Early Readers

When Hilda the hen goes out for the day,

Lenny the dog tries to get her to play.

'WOOF, WOOF!' he says, and she runs away.

Lenny just cannot get Hilda to stay.

C-DER™
CHEETAH Decodable & Early Readers

Once she gave Ken a peck on his nose,

when he tried to wet her with a hose.

He just wanted to give Hilda a bath,

but she wanted to get away from his path.

C-DER™
CHEETAH Decodable & Early Readers

11

She clucks each time she lays an egg,

and even when I beg and beg,

She does not let me have any;

she only shares her eggs with Mommy.

C-DER
CHEETAH Decodable & Early Readers
13

Now, there she is upon the hay.

'Have you any eggs today?' I say.

'Cluck,' she says, which means

'I do, but I do not have one for you'.

Discussion and activities:

1. Ask the children if they have every visited a chicken coop or pen. Have them share their experiences of what they saw there.

2. Have the children identify the words with the target letters and sounds.

3. Have the children make the sounds of the target letters and identify rhyming words in the text.

Discussion and activities:

4. Discuss the words *pen, weeds* and *hay* as used in the context of the story.

5. Have the children read the text aloud.

Questions:

1. Why do you think Hilda the hen does not fly as high or far as other birds?

....

2. What other things do hens eat besides what Hilda likes to eat?

....

www.ingramcontent.com/pod-product-compliance
Lightning Source LLC
Chambersburg PA
CBHW081306130726
47998CB00010B/2943